SHINE ON KING

The Guide to Being Your Best and Shaking the Haters

By

Gerard C McClure Jr

Table of Contents

FOREWORD

Examining the youth of today as they navigate through these truly turbulent times, it is important to prioritize sowing knowledge back into our communities so that same youth while traversing the adversities of life, has something to take with them. One of the most exciting and simultaneously scary moments in most of our young adult lives is the time after graduating high school. It's a time when they can reflect what a journey it's been and how they conquered the mountain. Despite the decreased societal "value" of it, we all know finishing high school is no easy task and when I say finish, I mean finishing high school in a good space mentally, emotionally and with ample potential future opportunities to progress through life.

The perils that a teenager faces as they steer themselves through the academics, social lives and personal rigors of the high school experience are all too well known. Learning how to balance academics, friendships, relationships, hormones, goal planning and the ever approaching "real world" successfully is an achievement worth celebrating. Hopefully every graduate reading this book has taken the proper time to acknowledge the work it took for them to cross that finish line. You all did it!

Now a brave new world awaits. As our youth plan for a life of unprecedented independence, I have little doubt that while excitement is there so are the questions; questions that they can find the answer to themselves. Questions that they will need help in answering. Questions that they don't even know they need to ask. Standing on the precipice of their first version of adulthood the most important thing I believe we can equip them with is experience rooted knowledge. We should also make that knowledge as diverse as possible.

While we all have wisdom to pour into our youth as they take this journey, our perspective is clearly limited. To create wisdom, we must give diversity. What we are unable to tell and to teach we must find those who can. Where we may be unfamiliar with situations, we must make sure that they get told about them in other ways.

This book and most importantly the author will be a valuable tool for the development of any young person reads it. Gerard has spent years developing young people academically, athletically and mentally. His work in the community speaks for itself and the desire to write this kind of book speaks to his character. While I am proud of him I am not all surprised.

I would come to know Gerard going into my senior year of high school when it was tradition for all of the upperclassmen football players with cars to pick up and drop off the underclassmen as we worked through summer workouts and training camp. My selection of Gerard at the time was merely based on proximity and I thought otherwise random. I would come to accept that such a decision was probably fate.

As Gerard was obviously a freshman in some of his ways, I was always impressed with his burgeoning leadership skills. Always relaxed, always focused and as a freshman starting at corner back on the varsity football team-the moments were never too big for him. As the season concluded and us seniors took stock of the future of the program his name was mentioned and agreed upon as one of the reasons it would be left in good hands.

As a kid myself I wasn't thinking about what kind of man I would become, let alone the kind of man he would become, but I will say that he has molded himself to be is no surprise to myself or anyone who knows him. His leadership, knowledge, compassion, concern, ability has been an asset to everybody who knows him and the city of St. Louis as a whole. If you or the young adult in your life hasn't had a chance to know Gerard personally now is the perfect chance to learn from somebody I would literally put in the life as a developer and mentor to my own child. We will all be better in particular our youth for having Gerard write this book. It should be a graduation present every year and on the shelf in every college dorm room.

Enjoy,

Michael Jones

Co-founder The Free Roots LLC

INTRODUCTION

'm from the Lou and I'm proud! The Lou is St Louis, Missouri in the Midwest of the United States if you're unfamiliar. Yes it's true that a lot of violence happens here each and every single day and night. The most positive thing I can pull from being born in a place that is far from picture perfect is that if you can make it here, you can make it anywhere. This has been one of the craziest years in the world to date and it's only June. Kobe Bryant was killed in a helicopter crash in January and I'm still shook over it. I know you're tired of being in the house having to listen to all the noise your family is making. The Coronavirus is up ticking again after America rushed a "re-opening" of all businesses and social gathering spots. It is my hope that you are being safe in all seriousness because people are really dying each and every single day. In the midst of all that Ahmad Arbury was killed jogging by three white men. I just saw on the news that a 7 year old black male was arrested in my city of St Louis for breaking into a home for burglary. Now I grew up around some future criminals but 7 years old the youngest I heard of since I been alive. Unemployment has gotten real rising to 38 million jobless citizens in the US strictly due to the coronavirus. The conversations about men in general media whether young or old is negative. Black men to be more specific and the lack of care we show our black women. Why this issue arose while we, as in black men, are being persecuted at a higher rate than ever before by way of public opinion is beyond me but that is a conversation for a different day. I know we are under scrutiny from every level. In these tough times remember these words I extend to you: Shine on King. According to Merriam Webster to shine means to perform extremely well. A King is one that holds a preeminent position especially a chief amongst competitors. Write those two definitions down and remember them as you read through this passage. I chose the lion because we all know that he is the king of the jungle and in this book, I will show you how to become the King of your life. Jay Z once said in the song Takeover "A wise man told me don't argue with fools, because people from a distance can't tell who is who". From this point on we are moving on from the fools and rolling with the winners in life. I want to you to adjust your mindset to 100% King Mode as you read through this. This is a conversation between me and you so take this as game given. After reading this I want you to apply it to your life during the summer and fall. Its time to step into a better version of you.

DREAM BIG KING

"We can transcend the script of a pre-defined story, and pave the way for the future that we design. We just need to tap that power, that conviction, that determination within us."

-Robert F Smith CEO of Vista Equity Partners 3 Billion Dollar Net worth

To be writing this is a dream come true. Confucius once said that "he who says he can and he who says he can't are both usually right." As a first time author I hope to provide encouragement and wisdom as you begin your journey to conquer your dreams. I have an important question for you that changed my whole life when it was asked to me. What would you be doing in life if you weren't afraid? Take some time and write down 5 things you would and don't restrict yourself during this time. Really think on this because it's an important step to building your kingdom. (5 Lines so that the reader can write down their ideas.

1: _____

2: _____

3:_____

4: _____

5: _____

I ask you all this because when it comes to dreaming big and wanting to impact the world, most of us are held hostage by our fears that keep us from exercising our natural god given talents. I'm no different from you or anybody else walking the streets, but I am a guy who decided to change my life from what I didn't want it to be and dream bigger. Here I am now, writing a book. At one point in my life I dropped out of college because I was tired of writing papers! You see, I don't even know you, but what I do know is that you have the power inside to make the world a better place.

The day we are born into this world we're given a certain timeframe to accomplish change in this world, in this country and in your environment that will affect the next few generations that come after you. Rather it's positive or negative is up to you. Go back to when you were a younger kid and think about when someone would ask you what you wanted to be when you grew up. I bet you didn't just tell them something you thought they wanted to hear. You told them exactly what you wanted to be, no matter how large your dream was. You knew in your mind how you wanted your life to go. As kids we're able to operate mentally without restriction but for some reason as we grow older, the world has a subtle way of diminishing your plans and visions.

To have a dream that no man has thought of you must have vision. Vision creates the start of the dream which moves you into action. You can think of this as a two step process. First you have the dream you have done all your exclusive thinking of the most amazing things you can do while alive. Next is the vision when you take that dream and start the process of bringing it into fruition. When it comes to your vision your must realize that you're thinking beyond the current moment we are in. Your vision must stretch your own belief of what you think can happen. The vision must include other people because you won't accomplish any of your dreams without the help of others.

Dreaming is the easiest thing to do, but they are also hard to accomplish. Sometimes people don't dream as big as they can and one thing about life is whatever you put your focus on the most usually becomes part of our life. So if you are reading this right now and don't have any big dreams or visions, find an activity to get the creative juices flowing, everybody wants to achieve something. Life can become more clear and fulfilling when you realize that anything can be accomplished if you set your mind to it and put in the due diligence.

Before we begin this journey into how you can start to dream bigger and start to make life how you want it, I first want you to do this exercise that helped me shift my life in a different direction. This may seem simple but I promise if you practice this activity daily when you wake and before you go to bed at night your mind will start to expand for the better. I want you to close your eyes and imagine that you're standing at the place you've always wanted to be with the people you want to be there.

Imagine being celebrated for accomplishing something you always wanted to do and the whole world is happy for your success. Don't hold back with where your imagination goes because that could hinder you from fully receiving the blessings God wants for you. Once you open your eyes I want you to go to the mirror and say with the greatest confidence, "I am worthy of success" five times. Right now you have done what many others have yet to do and that's claim your dream. Self-Affirmation is one key factor in achieving what you want in life as it activates your belief system.

In this world you have three types of people: those that win, those that lose, and those who haven't discovered how to win yet. The fact that you are reading this means you are committed to winning. Whatever situation you are going through right now whether good or bad I'm here to tell you things will get better. If no one has ever motivated you in a way you felt was real, I'm here to tell you that you can be the greatest ever. One important thing to know is that excuses only sound best to the people making them. You will hear many people in your life tell you things that they want to do but never get accomplished. I am guilty of doing this in my early 20's trying to do way too much at once. I don't want you being that person that can't deliver when it's time to perform. You may say "but you don't know what I'm going through" and my response to that is I won't pretend to know what you going through but what I do know is Philippians 4:13 says that you can do all things through Christ that strengthens you.

The Process of being KING

To have a great dream or vision is cool, but dreams without actions are wasted thoughts. So I will give you a 3 step plan that I know will help you ascend to the next level. Before we dive into that, I want you to take some time to write down 10 things you want to accomplish in the next 5 years. When you do this exercise, concentrate and focus on the future you want to be able to provide for yourself one day. Please don't limit yourself because that will ruin what you want to happen. This is your life and you must make it how you imagine it.

1: _____

2: _____

3: _____

4: _____

5: _____

6: _____

7: _____

8: _____

9: _____

10: _____

Writing down your goals is important in accomplishing your dreams which leads me to the 1st step in the process of being KING- the GAME PLAN. When it comes to game planning you have to be specific as possible. Knowing what you want is a key factor in accomplishing your dreams and vision. I remember hearing a great speaker share a mathematical equation that changed my way of looking at things and I will share it with you. WANTS+WHYS=MUST. Your why is what keeps your dream alive. For example when I started writing this in the beginning I had to figure out why I wanted to do it in the first place. I said to myself, someone out there is going through what I went through as a young man and I want to help prevent other young men from making any mistakes that I did. I wanted to make sure many young men like you coming after me will be ready to achieve success. The cause became bigger than me.

Making your dream bigger than you in the game planning session will put you in the right mind frame of paying it forward, an essential part of being a good human being. Another key component with you accomplishing your dreams and goals is setting dates to them. Putting dates to goals puts you in the right mindset to begin to execute the task at hand. This also shows assertiveness now that your have created a goal and a date behind it. You are now on your way to starting something great that will be both fulfilling and a contribution to the world.

The next step in the process of being KING is creating a GOOD CREW OF FRIENDS. There's a saying that I used to hear around the neighborhood growing up "If you hang around 9 people aren't doing anything with their life, guess who gone be number 10?" When it comes to accomplishing your dreams, you must surround yourself with people who are positive and want to do great things like you do. They must always hold you accountable and keep it the realist with you. You never want YES men around you that won't tell you when you're doing wrong or heading in the wrong direction. Those aren't real friends, I call them leaches just

trying to suck the life out of you. Yoι
begin to separate yourself from the f
potentially hinder you from reaching yʊ
even if you grew up with them. Surrounɑıɪg
yourself with people who are at your level or better
so you never stay in the same place is the best bet.
Not having this in your life will hold you back in the
long run.

Your crew of friends should always be
supportive of your dreams and visions even if they
aren't in the same field as you. Having those people
that support what you're doing even when other
outside people talk negative about you is very
important. They come in handy most when the
leaches gather and try to take your joy. Leaches
aren't always strangers, some of them will be in
your family. If you really want to accomplish your
dreams then you should make personal
connections with people who have successfully
done what you are aiming to do at the highest level.
Having an expert on your side that is willing to give
you advice is golden and will save you the time of
the mistakes they went through. What I want you to
do now is write down 5 successful people in the
field you want to be in no matter who it is. Follow
how they go about everything so you can take

ieces from all of them to become the best in your version.

1: _____

2: _____

3:_____

4: _____

5: _____

You have to surround yourself with success so you can develop success within yourself. This means you're ready for the final step to being KING- NEVER QUIT. This by far is the most important to remember if you ever want to accomplish your dreams. You must know that the journey to accomplishing your dreams is not an easy one by a long shot. As a matter of fact the bigger the dream the bigger the obstacles that will come your way. Those hard times will build you up and help you prevail in the end. God has a funny way of showing us it won't be easy by presenting failures in between accomplishments. Trust me, you will fail many times but the question is will you quit or figure out a way? To me that shows a big sign of growth when you begin to understand that overcoming failures will bring you closer to what god has for you. Trust me I know you will have those moments when it's just so tough you want to say forget it all, but that's when you have to remember your WHY and keep the faith. I've had many moments when I did quit but I got back in the game and it worked out for the better. No great success occurs overnight and even those people face trial and error.

If you know the story of Thomas Edison then you know he's a great example of not giving up or quitting. He failed a total of 10,000 times attempting to invent the lighting bulb and on 10,001 he finally got it. Imagine if he would have stopped at 10,000 you and I would be sitting in dark rooms with candles to read this. Is your dream worth trying it again and again even after you have failed time after time? Will you give up on your dreams when people tell you it is impossible? If you said yes just reevaluate what you're doing and then come back and answer no.

My brother let me leave you with some encouraging words straight from the heart. You have been a natural born winner since birth. Think about it, of all the millions of sperm cells that could have made it you your mom's egg you were the one to make it through. That's god way of letting you know that there is a place on earth for you to accomplish your dreams. You are the greatest person to ever live and you must have that type of confidence daily. You must believe what you are doing is necessary for the world to see and be affected by it. People are born into this world but live dying everyday because they are not living out their dream. You have the power within to create the life you want to have, but you must believe you can do it.

I believe in you while you may not believe in yourself, because I know anything is possible. I doubted myself a lot in the process of making this, but many believed in me to finish this and here we are. You are always one step closer to getting where you want to go long as you never give up on your dreams. Stay strong my brother and I hope to meet you one day and hear how you have changed the world with your talents. Shine On KING.

BONUS CHAPTER

GRADUATION BLVD:

CHANGE THE GAME, CREATE EXCELLENCE

CHAPTER 1:

NEW MIND, NEW HABIT

"As I see it today, the ability to read awoke in me some long dormant craving to be mentally alive."

– Malcolm X

Invest in Personal Development

It's finally arrived, that moment when you're about to take the first step into adulthood and depart from under your parents' roof. It's time to deliver on all the great things you said you'd do after high school and everybody is watching, waiting on you to succeed or fail. This is what it's all about and you must remember that everything you do from here has an impact on your future as well as those around you. There will undoubtedly be pressure and in most instances, more than you've ever felt before. To succeed, you must not let that pressure overwhelm you. See it as a formality. What I mean is, look at the pressure as a natural occurrence. No matter who you are, going out on your own for the first time after high school has ended will be accompanied by this same pressure. It is just the hope and dreams that you want to live up to reminding you of your purpose. That pressure is the aspirations and accomplishments everyone else around you want you to conquer. Part of it is wanting you to be a good example for the younger kids, part of it is your folks wanting to brag about you to everybody. Like many who embark on post high school educational journeys, you were probably the man at your high school or maybe you weren't, but even still, the next level of your conquest is here. The homeboys can't accompany you through this as they did the previous stage. Walking on campus beating your chest as if you've seen it all and done it all which most adolescent young black men tend to do as a natural response to a new environment, often result in some of the worst life lessons that can be learned through far less painful experiences. It's not worth your time nor the reputation you think you want which always turns out to be very short lived. Don't be afraid of what's to come because every man's journey differs from the next with its own intricate twist and turns. The result of this particular stage that should be the primary aim is graduation. Whether you attend an in-state or out of state college the steps remain the same: be where you supposed to be, do what you're supposed to do. 1st thing I want to tell you is focus on the top 5 schools you want to go to and not the ones that will accept you. What I mean by that is, a lot of time guidance counselors and others around you will have their opinions of where it is they think you should attend. I'm here to tell you there is nothing worse than listening to another's advice on what university to spend the next 4-5 years of your life at and you get off that plane or to the end of that car ride and think, "what the hell am I doing here." Although, you probably will think that for a second anyway even when following through on your own choice of university. Most colleges are looking for high GPAs, high test scores, and great resumes/-recommendations to justify offering you big scholarship money. If you're not able to get a full scholarship that's no reason to completely count yourself out. Do your due diligence early in the beginning of your sophomore and junior year of high school to see what scholarships you can get with the GPA and test score you have. Make sure to stay in constant contact with all guidance counselors who are placed in your HS to help you with such a huge decision. Describing college, I'll say it's a period of discovering your passion to a degree that you're able to expound upon it and communicate what it is you take from that, to the rest of the world. Now just because you've vacated the nest, doesn't mean there aren't rules. Institutional rules. Rules to abide by to keep your scholarship or to stay in school period. You will have the freedom to do what you want because it's just you, but if I've learned anything in life, it's the things we do and the decisions we make when there's no one else around, that largely shape our habits and lives later on down the road. Your intentions entering college should be to make the best grades, have fun, and graduate while trying to impact the environment you live in. Everything you want out of college is attainable no matter what anybody says. Depending on your family income you may have to take out student loans. There are other feasible options. Option 1: If your test scores are great meaning over 25 ACT, grade point average is high meaning 3.5/above, and recommendations are strong then apply to your dream school. Have at least 5 to 10 schools on the list to choose from. Some of your dream schools may not accept you and that's being real. Why else would they be your dream school if the just admitted anyone right? Thousands of people from across the world are applying to school daily so universities here in the US have what they like to call selective student picking and limited room. Don't be afraid to apply to the school's people say you can't get into. As I said in the intro anything is possible if you believe. Option 2 is if you don't have the grades or test scores to get in your dream school, but still want to go there in the future. You don't want to start off with student loan debt like I did leaving college so you can save up some money and go to a junior college in your hometown. This way is cheaper and you can get most of the same general courses there that you would've taken your freshmen and sophomore years at a big university. While there you can get a high-grade point average and get a transfer scholarship to your dream school and receive other scholarships available for you. The less loan debt you have while in college, the better it is to graduate and live life on your own terms. Say if you're reading and think "I don't want to go to neither I want to do construction or be an electrician etc." For you there are many trade schools out there that you can attend and get your certification and start making big bank using your skill to help with consumer problems. When choosing a major, make sure it is helping you reach your purpose in life. Don't choose a major that someone wanted you to do unless that person is doing what you strive to be in the future. It can be stressful being in a major that you don't want to be in knowing that you should be doing something else. If you're unsure of what you want to choose just go undecided for a semester or two to figure it out. Make sure your family is financially educated on what it will cost to go to your school and how it will be paid for. These are the first two topics that should be discussed before the process even takes place. What you are about to experience this fall or spring will be a new phase to create a better you. Don't go in not knowing anything about what you're there for because you will get sent home just as fast as you came. You are going there to change your life and become the greatest you. Building a strong foundation in your first year with a good grade point average and no disciplinary issues on campus will create momentum for you moving forward in the rest of your college days please believe me when I say that.

A Long Way Home- From the Lou to the Gump

I remember when I found out I was going to Alabama State University on a scholarship I was super excited. Getting to that point was a tough one because my senior year in high school didn't go how I wanted it to. I had to swallow a tough pill that I wasn't going to get a football scholarship to college. I didn't live up to the hype and our record for that season wasn't good. All my friends were getting scholarships for football while I just watched and congratulated. At that time of my life all I wanted to do was to get a football scholarship like my friends not even realizing the other talents God had blessed me with. This sent me into a great depression because I know I was talented, but I was in desperation mode to get a scholarship on the football field. I started taking steroids after the season to get bigger because I knew I was too light in weight for big division 1 schools to want to recruit me. I was trying to prove a point to myself that I could do it and quiet the naysayers. Now I did get bigger once I started taking the steroids, but the side effects had its impact on me. My grades in the first two quarters of senior year were terrible because my focus was not there at all. I changed so much in a negative way that I couldn't even recognize myself. It took a life or death situation with my mom for me to take life seriously and I decided that I would get off the steroids because it was affecting the people closest to me. My final two quarters I wasn't on any drugs or substances and handled my business which resulted in me graduating in May of 2007. Originally, I was going to attend Tuskegee University founded by the great Booker T. Washington. They had a cool computer science summer program I had been accepted in that I was going to use to get a scholarship there as well and major in computer science. I was just glad to be accepted into college so I could prove my worth to myself. In the process of that happening my football coach/mentor found a scholarship at Alabama State University I qualified for with my grade point average that paid for room plus board. Obviously I pulled the trigger on the latter opportunity. That taught me an early lesson about keeping the faith and believing in myself no matter what. It was the best thing that could happen for me because my mom wouldn't have to come out of pocket for my education. I was going down there with two of my closes high school classmates, so I knew I wouldn't be the only one down there from St. Louis and I had some people that had my back in the unfortunate case that an unsavory scenario arose. My family and close friends were proud of me, so I was confident and didn't need validation from a soul. I remember having one of the biggest going away parties that summer of 2007. My girlfriend and I at the time had decided we were going to keep the relationship going through college, so I was hyped up with my nose open. Leaving for Alabama was cool because I was going somewhere out of my comfort zone which was needed for my growth. That drive down to Montgomery felt like the longest 8 hours ever. When we pulled up on campus, I couldn't believe what I was seeing. It was so many beautiful girls just walking in every direction of the campus. I was used to always being around and interacting with the pretty ladies in high school, but to see girls from Atlanta, California, Florida and Alabama fine to and have that southern hospitality I heard about, I was in love already. The freshmen summer orientation weekend was off the chain. I just knew I met my wife 50 different times. How could the universe do this to me knowing I had a girl going to Ohio for college? My roommate I had that was from Tuscaloosa,

Alabama had put me on to Lil Boosie and the down south music, so I got hipped fast to the culture down there. Before I returned for the fall I made a promise to myself that I would not be the one to be returning home at the end of the semester because I could not let my mom down. I came in majoring in computer science because I was told it would make me a lot of money. I went with that not knowing I would be taking classes in subjects that never interest me which was science and math. I'm not saying anything bad about the two subjects, I just have never been a fan of all those formulas because they make my brain hurt. That first semester was rough. I was in class always confused because most of my teachers were foreign and their accents were crazy to me. The only two classes I was passing that semester were English and this personal development class. They had fit the things I enjoyed growing up. My English professor Ms. Margaret Holler Stephens was a cool lady. She was unique to me because she also was in a book as a teacher which is something I hadn't seen before in school. I could learn the English language in a cool way and write a lot. My professional development class was cool because the professor got us too really think about out futures which allowed me to start dreaming again. During it all I was a party animal every week and it cost me at the worst times. I was going out Tuesday and Thursday nights knowing I had advanced math at 8am the next morning, but I had to do my thing so I was drinking too much with no regards for time. Mind you I'm not even 21 so I shouldn't have been drinking anyway. Suddenly you wake up and its 11am and realize you've missed all your classes that day. Yeah I went hard like that at times and in my mind I thought I was holding it together but in reality I was sinking fast in the classroom. Campus life was crazy and that freshmen class in the fall of 2007 at Alabama State was one of the greatest ever. The band was always booming with the music across the street every night so it was always live. I remember getting to perform with the sorority Zeta Phi Beta at the homecoming step show and we won so big up to Nicole Bonner in Dubai for looking out for me. The first time I got to see Cornell West speak was in the Acadome top row for free which was crazy because I had always wanted to hear him speak in high school. I even got to sit in the bus where Rosa Park sat when she was arrested. That moment for me was everlasting. With the end of the semester coming I was frustrated because I knew I wasn't performing well in the classroom and I didn't like the major I was in anymore which put my scholarship in immediate danger. When final exams came I did like every college last minute slacker and tried to turn it on. I was studying harder than I ever had before. I took my finals exams with confidence and returned home for Christmas break with even more confidence. I'll never forget when my grades came in the mail. I was sitting in the kitchen when my mom walks in the kitchen with mail from the school. From the looks of it I thought it was a refund check, but when she opened it the look on her face said it all. I was scared to even say anything as she brought the wrath of God on me with many profound words. My grade point average was bad and to be on scholarship I knew I had messed up big time. I took it upon myself to change because when you know you are responsible for what happened it gives you a better perspective. So, the spring semester I changed my major to theatre. It was the best decision I had made since being in college. I took more interests in my classes and I was more focused because I didn't want to repeat last semesters' results. At the end of that spring my grades were better and I was making a comeback. I returned to St. Louis for the summer ready to have the time of my life, but that was short lived. About a week later I get a letter from Alabama State and I was too nervous to open it. I sat with it for an hour before my nerves would allow me to pick it up again. When I open it my stomach dropped because all I saw on that letter was that I had lost my scholarship. My cumulative grade point average was not even close to what was required. Making that call to my mom while she was at work had my heart jumping through my shirt. Once I told her you would have thought she was standing right next to me the way her voice was coming through that phone. I had made a promise to her that I didn't keep and that hurt the worse. I knew she couldn't afford to pay for my school tuition and I lost the only thing that could keep that from happening. I felt like I had let the world down. I could have returned for summer school to try to make it up, but I was mentally out of it by then and decided not to return. That summer was one that would change my life forever.

Personal Development

"How you gone win if you aint right within?" That's a classic line by one of the greatest rappers ever by the name of Lauryn Hill. There's no better place to start then with the man in the mirror as Michael Jackson would say. You hold the key to your destiny and nobody else. The success you will see in your lifetime is all about the person you become in the process. We look at the superstars and see all the material things they have and think that it just happened overnight, but without the personal development those folks would not be where they are today. There comes a time in your life where you must say to yourself "this is it." You will realize that your life is worth more than what you see in the present and this is where life will begin to take off. You must understand that you are on a journey of spreading your talent and knowledge to the world in whatever way God put it in you to do so. There's an audio by Earl Nightingale called The Strangest Secret and in that is a line that says "you are what you think about." Now you may not understand this right now, but that means everything. Our minds are so powerful and control so much of what we do. Using your mind to think about negative things will affect your life tremendously. The world in general doesn't promote a lot of positive things especially about black men and boys. We must break through this barrier as early as we can. Being in control of self is being in control of your life. Another thing in personal development is self-belief. This is the 1st key to success. There is great power in believing in yourself because it ties into faith which comes from a higher power. The greatest successes to ever live had to believe in themselves to reach their dreams and you're no different. The possibilities are endless to the person who knows it can be done. Continuing to become a better you everyday increases confidence which in return will increase self-belief and you'll start to accomplish amazing things. Look at it like this, if you were living your dream right now how would that person be acting right now? Knowing what your vision looks like is very important to taking control of your life which brings me into creating a vision board for yourself. I know you've heard of the phrase seeing is believing; well your vision board will help you to believe more every day. When creating the vision board you want to have the things you want to have in the future. This could be that degree, a company you want to start, that Ferrari you been dreaming about driving or just anything you have always dreamed about having. Don't limit yourself with this process, but use it to help you stretch your mind to limitless possibilities. First get you a big poster board from the store. Then you can search the web for the images you want to print and cut out. Make sure you're vision board is positioned somewhere that you can see it when you wake up and before you go to bed.

The most important thing you need to know for success in the classroom is to stay proactive because your professors don't have to tell you everything that will be on a quiz or test. It is your responsibility to always be knowledgeable of what is being taught. You should always be asking questions in class as well to show the professor you want to learn. Professors respect students who take initiative to do more than is taught in class. Always build great relationships with them because they are your ticket to getting out of school and into post graduate schools if that's the route you want to take after getting your bachelors. I know you probably have heard this before but sitting in the front of the class really is beneficial. 1st the teacher sees you which is very important if the class size is big. This can be the difference between you getting the help you need from the professor. Another good thing is most of the A students sit in the first two rows so even if you can't understand what the professor is saying you will have a student next to you who knows what's going on and will help if you are putting forth effort.

When it comes to getting your books for the semester, make sure you always are checking the book websites online to find the cheapest book. The bookstores on campus can get out of hand sometimes with the prices so I'm a big fan of paying less. A few I recommend are Book Renter, Chegg.com, Textbook.com, and Half.com. This part is very important because you will have some teachers who will expect you to do readings and assignments from the beginning and will not accept any excuses. Ask around if you don't know, but don't spend hundreds of dollars when you can pay way less. One thing that will always keep your journey through college successful is to stay true to yourself. You are in there to grow as an individual while learning a specific interest that can change the world. It's so easy to get caught up with what other people are doing that you end up losing your own vision.

There are a few key people on campus that you should build good relationships with. The first is the Dean of your department and the whole staff. If you have strong relationships with the whole department you will get strong letters of recommendations to graduate school that could go a long way. They want you to succeed but you must meet them halfway. The second group is the people in the student accounting office. Financial aid offices are filled with angry students every day so the people in there need a positive vibe no matter what the situation is to get your needs solved. The last groups are the people that work in the library and writing labs. You will have tons of college papers to construct so making good relationships with these group will be very beneficial. Most professors will make you use APA format for your papers so having someone who can help with the process will help tremendously no matter the class. With these key relationships, you will always be aware of what's going on and succeed every semester. You should always be keeping up with how many hours you have attempted and hours you have passed throughout your college years because schools have certain limits on how many hours you can attempt before they dismiss you from the university. What I want you to do now take a minute to write down your top three goals for the school year below. What you have just done is something most of the top successful people in the world do and that's put their goals to paper. You have set yourself apart from the rest before you even touch campus ground. Once your path is set, it's hard for you to steer off the track. The story of the all-time great Marcus Garvey is an example of this.

Story of Marcus Garvey.

Marcus Mosiah Garvey, one of the most influential 20th Century Black Nationalist and Pan-Africanist leaders, was born on August 17, 1887 in St. Ann's Bay, Jamaica. Greatly influence by Booker T. Washington's autobiography *Up From Slavery*, Garvey began to support industrial education, economic separatism, and social segregation as strategies that would enable the assent of the "black race." In 1914, Garvey established the Universal Negro Improvement Association (UNIA) in Kingston, Jamaica, adopting Washington's inspirational phrase "Up, you mighty race; you can conquer what you will." By May of 1917, Garvey relocated the UNIA in Harlem and began to use speeches and his newspaper, The *Negro World*, to spread his message across the United States to an increasingly receptive African American community. His major audience included the thousands of Southern blacks who were then migrating from the "shadow of slavery and the plantation" to the urban North. Black veterans of World War I were another Garvey audience. Most of them had experienced both French equality and US military bigotry and returned home as militant "race men." They were attracted to Garvey's calls. The UNIA grew larger still following the race riots in the <u>Red Summer of 1919</u>. But Garvey knew African Americans would not take action if they did not change their perceptions of themselves. He hammered home the idea of racial pride by celebrating the African past and encouraging African Americans to be proud of their heritage and proud of the way they looked. Garvey proclaimed "black is beautiful" long before it became popular in the 1960s. He wanted African Americans to see themselves as members of a mighty race. "We must canonize our own saints, create our own martyrs, and elevate to positions of fame and honor black men and women who have made their distinct contributions to our racial history." He encouraged parents to give their children "dolls that look like them to play with and cuddle," and he did not want black people thinking of themselves in a defeatist way. "I am the equal of any white man; I want you to feel the same way."

Knowing what you want in life will make it so much better. In chapter one you saw how to prepare for your year of college and how personal development will help you move to a higher level. In the next chapter I will show you how having a mastermind team gets you one step closer to Graduation Blvd.

Made in the USA
Columbia, SC
16 September 2020

20363377R00029